THE BODY
Purity

written by
Monica Ashour

designed by
David Fiegenschue & Emily Gudde

Level 8

BOOK 1

Second Edition

TOBET THEOLOGY OF THE BODY EVANGELIZATION TEAM

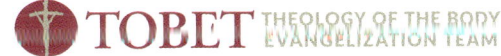

Dedicated to the Church, including our family and friends, and especially to Mother Mary and Saint John Paul.

Tremendous thanks to all TOBET members over the years. Special thanks to Alyssan, Colleen, Erika, Kathy, Lisa, Luke, Mike, Patrick, Robin, Sheryl, and Véronique. We are grateful for consultation work by the translator of the *Theology of the Body*, Dr. Michael Waldstein, as well as Dr. Susan Waldstein. We are also grateful for the consultation work of Katrina J. Zeno, MTS.

For the Golden Sessioners

Nihil Obstat: Tomas Fuerte, S.T.L.
Censor Librorum

Imprimatur: +Most Reverend Samuel J. Aquila, S.T.L.
Archbishop of Denver
Denver, Colorado, USA
October 8, 2018

Library of Congress information on file. ISBN 978-1-945845-38-3 • Second Edition

Cover Design: FigDesign • Layout: Emily Gudde • Editor: Dayspring Brock • Associate Editor: Alexis Mausolf

Excerpts from the English translation of the *Catechism of the Catholic Church*. New York: Catholic Book Publishing Co., 1994.

Based on John Paul II's *Man and Woman He Created Them: A Theology of the Body*. Trans. Michael Waldstein, Copyright © 2006. Used by permission of Pauline Books & Media, 50 Saint Paul's Ave, Boston, Massachusetts 02130. All rights reserved. www.pauline.org.

The quote on p. 35 is John Paul II. "Letter to Families." *Holy See*, Feb. 2, 1994, w2.vatican.va/content/john-paul-ii/en/letters/1994/documents/hf_jp-ii_let_02021994_families.html.

The quote on p. 39 is John Paul II. "Redemptor Hominis." *Holy See*, Mar. 4, 1979, w2.vatican.va/content/john-paul-ii/en/encyclicals/documents/hf_jp-ii_enc_04031979_redemptor-hominis.html.

The quote on p. 45 is John Paul II. "Homily of His Holiness John Paul II." The Holy See. Rome, Oct. 6, 1979, para. 4, https://w2.vatican.va/content/john-paul-ii/en/homilies/1979/documents/hf_jp-ii_hom_19791006_washington-san-matteo.html.

All Scripture verses are from the *New American Bible*, Revised Edition (NABRE).

Printed in the United States of America. © Copyright 2021 Monica Ashour. All rights reserved. No part of this book may be reproduced or transmitted in any form or by any means, electronic or mechanical, including photocopying, recording, or by any information storage and retrieval system without permission in writing from the publisher.

Table of Contents

1. Real vs. Counterfeit — 4
- The gift of self is giving, receiving, and open to others.
- The language of the body is to be spoken in truth.
- Holiness means that bodily actions follow the promptings of a well-formed heart.

2. Chemistry and Love — 16
- Attraction is God-given and meant to propel us toward real love.
- Sin begins in the heart, but God can purify the heart.
- Viewing others as brothers and sisters is a good preparation for marriage.

3. The Sacred One-Flesh Union — 24
- Giving, receiving, and fruitfulness is the pattern for marital love.
- It is important to notice the inner movements of the heart.
- Friendship is a good preparation for real love in marriage.

4. Identity and Vocation — 38
- Purity gives us the freedom to love and be loved.
- True freedom is living according to God's design, which leads to real love.
- Jesus and Mary love freely, fully, faithfully, and fruitfully.

1 Real vs. Counterfeit

Priceless or Worthless?

If you had a choice between a real $100 bill or a counterfeit $1,000 bill, which would you choose? The $1,000 seems bigger and better, but in reality, only the $100 has monetary value. The real is always better than the counterfeit.

Significantly more important than money is love. We are often enticed by counterfeit "love", but **real** love is the most satisfying. You could put it this way: counterfeit love is worthless, and real love… priceless.

So how do we know if love is real or counterfeit? Counterfeit love may seem like the real thing, but underneath, it is selfish and unsatisfying. Real love, on the other hand, wants the good of the other person, because it is sacrificial.

What is Love?

Real Love	Counterfeit Love
Sacrificial	Selfish
Decision-centered	Feelings-centered
Long-suffering	Impatient
Total	Partial
Forgiving	Unforgiving
Priceless	Worthless

© Copyright 2018 by Monica Ashour. All rights reserved.

The Truth of the Body

Recognizing real love among its many counterfeits is not as easy as it sounds. St. John Paul offers a clue to understanding the difference: the **body**. More precisely, we can know real love when we understand the true meaning of the body.

St. John Paul developed what he called the Theology of the **Body**—not the theology of the **soul**, not the theology of the **spirit**, not even the theology of **love**. Why the body? The body has a deep meaning; the body is a sign of a whole person whom God created for love. Unfortunately, the body has been misunderstood in modern times.

Many people inaccurately view the body as an empty shell or avatar in which the spirit is trapped. They allow themselves to be governed by fleeting feelings, without taking into account God's design of the human person. Even Christians who believe in the Incarnation sometimes forget that the body is important. But St. John Paul reminds us that the body matters!

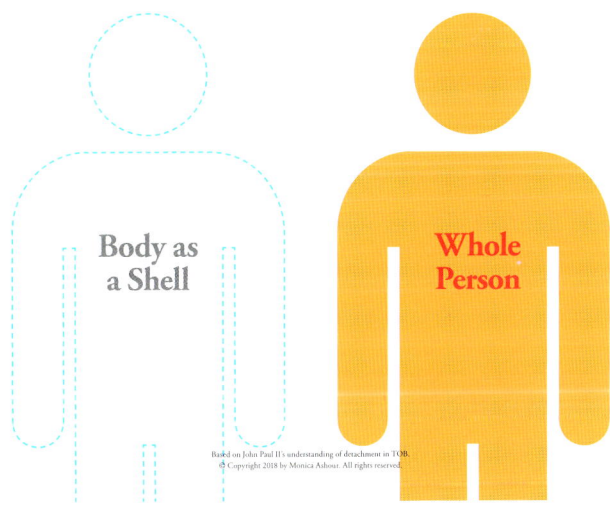

Let's discuss the deeper meaning of the body by looking at **three fundamental truths** of Theology of the Body.
- Real love is the gift of self.
- The body speaks a language.
- Holiness begins with the heart.

5

The Imprint of Love

When searching for a definition of real love, where better to start than God Himself? What is the nature of God? Scripture says, "God is love" (1 John 4:8), even before the universe was created. Since love can never be solitary, God must be more than one Person.

Indeed, God is not only one Person but three Persons: God the Father, God the Son, and God the Holy Spirit united in real love from all eternity. The Trinity is a communion of three Persons in one complete union.

God's Love is marked by giving, receiving, and openness to an Other. The Father gives the Gift of Himself to the Son, Who receives the Father's Gift. The Son, in turn, gives the Gift of Himself to the Father. This giving and receiving is life-giving: the eternal, uncreated Holy Spirit is the actual bond between the Father and Son.

God's Inner Life of Love

Based on idea by Dr. Margaret Turek. © Copyright 2018 by Monica Ashour. All rights reserved.

God created the universe, and so the giving-receiving-fruitful pattern, or imprint, of His nature is reflected all around us. For example, plants give us oxygen, and we give them carbon dioxide, resulting in sustained life for all. Notice even in the body, one person's vocal cords give while another's eardrums receive; communication is the result.

And this is the same model for real love. Even the family and the Church are marked by this imprint, as shown below. When we model our lives, communities, and relationships on this pattern, we are mirroring the very nature of our Creator. Through the **gift of self**—love—we image God the most.

God's Imprint of Love on the Universe

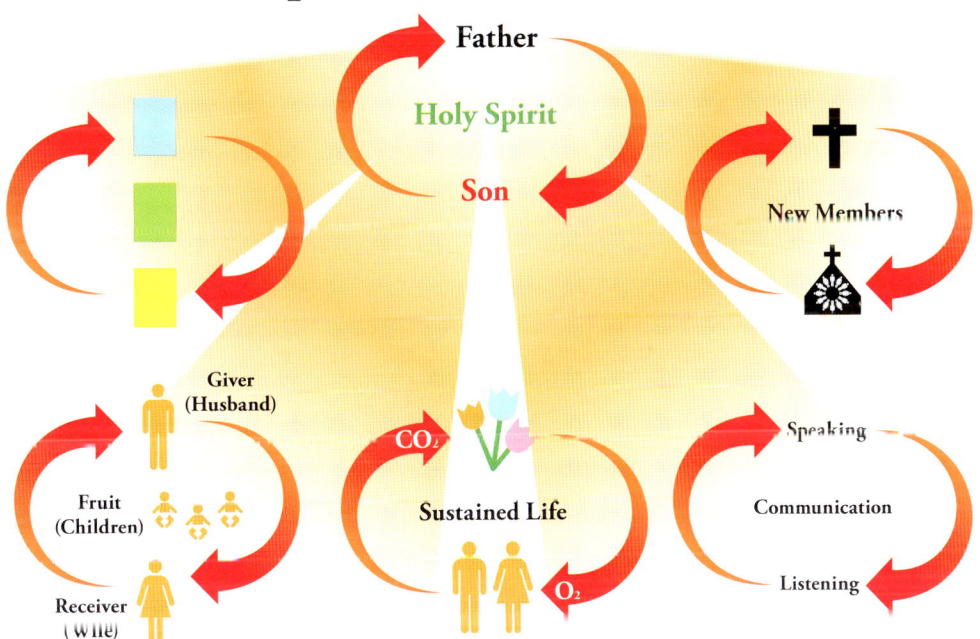

© Copyright 2020 by Monica Ashour. All rights reserved.

Real Love Is the Gift of Self

Love is giving, love is receiving, and love is open to others. In relationships, there is constant giving and receiving. Our very bodies are directed toward each other. How can we make gifts of self?
- With your lips, you might kiss your mom as she drops you off at school. This is a gift of self.
- With your legs, you might walk to the water fountain to fill your teacher's water bottle. This is also a gift of self.

Real love means **giving**.

But there's more. Love is not only giving; it is also receiving.
- With your ears, you can actively listen to your friend's funny story, even though you may have heard it before. That is a gift of self.
- With your eyes, you might watch your sister pitching at her softball game and appreciate her talent, even when you are hot and tired sitting on the bleachers. This is a gift of self.

Real love means **receiving**.

Mutual giving and receiving bring closeness, trust, laughter, and appreciation. This is the fruitfulness of relationship. Real love is **life-giving**.

The Body Says, "I Am A Gift"

The Gift of Self
GIVING and RECEIVING for FRUITFULNESS

Based on TOB 13:4. © Copyright 2018 by Monica Ashour. All rights reserved.

"[Using] turns [a person] into an object of manipulation."
Theology of the Body 123:1

Love vs. Use

To understand how love is the gift of self, we might ask about its counterfeit. What is the opposite of love? You may be tempted to say "hate," and it is true that hatred is destructive to relationships. But St. John Paul emphasizes that the opposite of love is actually something else: **use**. This is when one person sees another as an object to be used, not a gift to be loved. If using someone masquerades as love, this "love" is counterfeit. Can you think of some examples when "giving" is actually use?

- What if you gave your mom a kiss—but only to get some allowance money? That is a form of use.
- Or what if you filled your teacher's water bottle in hopes that she might give you a better grade? That is a form of use.

Can "receiving" also be a form of use?

- What if you listened to your friend's story only to make fun of him in front of others? That is a form of use.
- What if you went to your sister's softball game only to point out all her errors and make yourself look good? That is a form of use.

To avoid use, first be aware that it is the opposite of love. It is true that our motives are not always selfless, but we can work to purify our motives and practice real love.

9

The Body Speaks a Language

The next basic Theology of the Body principle is that the **body speaks a language**. What does that mean? It means that we can "speak" the truth of love not only with words but also with bodily actions. Think of it this way: **certain bodily actions mean certain things.** Of course, some gestures vary according to time period and culture, but there is a basic truth to human actions which is easy to interpret.

- What is the meaning of a hug?
  You open your arms when you are welcoming and trusting.
- What is the meaning of a punch?
  You use your fists when you are defending yourself.
- What is the meaning of a frown?
  Your mouth and eyes move downward when you are unhappy.

Our body's actions should be truthful to their God-given meanings; that's called integrity. We feel wronged when we know a bodily action has been robbed of its God-given meaning.

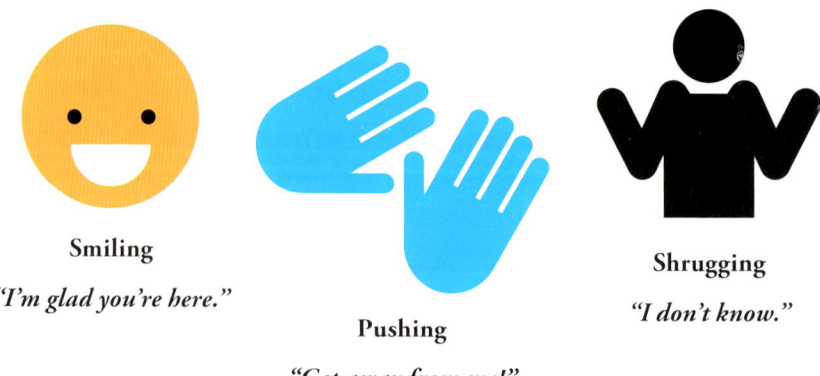

The Body Speaks a Language
There is meaning behind every bodily action

Smiling
"I'm glad you're here."

Pushing
"Get away from me!"

Shrugging
"I don't know."

Based on the significance of the term, "Detachment from the meaning of the body," especially in *TOB* 123:1, *TOB* 125:1; *TOB* 127:1; *Humanae Vitae* 13.
© Copyright 2018 by Monica Ashour. All rights reserved.

It is possible to tell a lie with the body. For instance, laughter is meant to bond people. Laughing with someone is unifying. However, laughing **at** someone rather than **with** someone causes division, and the body tells a lie.

Many sins fall into the category of telling a lie with the body. Cheating is telling a lie with the body. Gossiping is telling a lie with the body. Disobeying parents or teachers is telling a lie with the body. As you go through your day, ask yourself: "Am I telling the truth with my body?"

Counterfeit "Kindness"

A few middle-school boys decided to play a prank on Joseph, a shy student in their class. Before lunch, they mixed ketchup into some pudding and offered it to him, pretending to be kind. Joseph took one bite and then spit it out, more hurt by the betrayal of his friends than he was by the offensive pudding. His friends told a lie with their bodies since their "kindness" was counterfeit.

"While the powers [of sin tend to separate] the 'language of the body' from the truth, that is, try to falsify it, the power of love, by contrast, strengthens it ever anew in that truth...."   *Theology of the Body 127:1*

Holiness Begins with the Heart

Our final Theology of the Body concept deals with the importance of the body and **holiness**, and it may surprise you. Many of us think holiness means never having fun. But this is a counterfeit understanding of real holiness. Real holiness means this: **the truth that you know is the truth you should show**.

Let's write that as a math problem:

Pure Heart + Matching Bodily Action = Holiness

So how do we get a **pure** heart? First, we need to know the definition of purity. *Purity* means that there is no contamination. In other words, you know what is right, and you are not tainted by the counterfeit. A well-formed conscience helps you to know right from wrong. Your heart is formed by your parents, the Bible, the Church, and God Himself.

Here is the harder part: once you know what is right in your pure heart, then your bodily actions are to reflect this knowledge. This integrity is possible when you rely on God's grace. Holiness is related to wholeness.

12

You know in your pure heart that you should spend time with your little brother and sister.

With your bodily action, you create a fun game that you all will enjoy.

Holiness

You know in your pure heart you should not cheat on your math test.

With your bodily action, you work out your own calculations, keeping your eyes on your own paper.

Holiness

To be holy is to be whole. Holiness is deciding day-to-day and minute-to-minute to do what you know is right, body and heart together. A wholly holy heart is God's will for you!

The Diminished Heart

Since holiness is pure heart and body working in accord, then what is the opposite of holiness? When you "split" your body from your spirit, this detachment creates a rupture; it is the division of your body from your heart. In other words, to detach your body from your pure heart is called sin.

Splitting your bodily actions from the truth in your heart, or your well-formed conscience, leads to sin. Here it is expressed as a new math problem:

Pure Heart + **Detached Bodily Action** = **Sin**

Not only does sin hurt your relationship with God and your relationships with others—it hurts you.

You know in your pure heart that you should be reverent during Mass.

With your bodily action, you get your phone out and text during the Liturgy.

Sin

You know in your pure heart that telling a lie is wrong.

With your bodily action, you claim that you lost your homework, when actually, you never completed it.

Sin

"So for one who knows the right thing to do and does not do it, it is a sin." Jas. 4:17

Understanding the Heart

Let's explore the heart a bit more. St. John Paul says we are mature when we become aware of the "inner movements of the heart" and then evaluate them. Being aware of the "inner movements" means noticing our subtle desires and feelings. Then we need to evaluate those motives and feelings and purify them.

For instance, you notice in the inner movements of your heart that you want to get to know someone.

Now, evaluate that desire by asking yourself, "What are my motives?"
- If, in your heart, you want to make this person feel accepted and involved...
- If, in your heart, you want to get to know and build a friendship with that person...
   ...then with your bodily actions, go for it!

Immature Heart

"If I cheated, I would save time and make all A's."

"I'd really like to gossip about her and what she did at school."

"I wonder if people would like me more if I posted my friend's secret on social media."

Not Identifying Impulses + Not Evaluating Impulses = *Immaturity*

Based on Mt 5:8, 27-28 and *TOB* 48:3. © Copyright 2018 by Monica Ashour. All rights reserved.

On the other hand:
- If, in your heart, you are planning to use this person for your own popularity...
- If, in your heart, you desire to demean, bully, or gossip about that person...
   ...then with your bodily actions, resist!

14

Maturing Heart

"If I cheated, I would save time and make all A's."
"Hmm. It would be better if I saved time by choosing to study instead of playing video games."

"I'd really like to gossip about her and what she did at school."
"Why did I think that? Maybe I'm jealous of her."

"I wonder if people would like me more if I posted my friend's secret on social media."
"Wait… I may be using my friend to get attention."

Identifying Impulses + Evaluating Impulses = *Maturity*

Based on Mt 5:8, 27-28 and *TOB* 48:3. © Copyright 2018 by Monica Ashour. All rights reserved.

Notice from the diagram on this page that mature people are still tempted to sin, but they catch themselves and choose real love instead. Temptation is an inclination to divide body from heart. The Holy Spirit helps us to live purely, and mature people listen to His promptings and work to match their bodily actions to their pure hearts.

The path to maturity is not always smooth; we all stumble sometimes. In those cases, the Sacrament of Reconciliation is the best way to get back on track. It re-unifies your body and heart; moreover, it reconciles you with God.

Points to Ponder:
1. What are the three basic Theology of the Body concepts introduced in this lesson? Give one real example of each.
2. What is true maturity? What are some steps you can take to become more mature?

Mission: Become aware of your heart's purity. At the end of the day, look back and find one moment when your bodily actions didn't match up with your pure heart. Ask God to help you to mature, and tomorrow work on making sure your bodily actions match your pure heart.

15

2 Chemistry and Love

Opposites Attract

The previous chapter covered three basic truths of Theology of the Body. When you are guided by the truth of the gift of self, the language of the body, and holiness, you are living out purity—the integrity of the body and spirit together. Now, let's build on that foundation for a healthy and holy view of sexuality.

The first thing for you to know is that God created attraction, and whatever God creates is good. This good attraction between a woman and a man draws them closer to each other in wonder and awe, possibly leading to marriage.

The body teaches us that we are meant to go toward an "other." Boy meets girl, and girl meets boy. There is chemistry! The word *chemistry* is used for a reason. Think of what you've learned in your science classes about attraction.

In an atom, protons attract electrons. This attraction is the basic building block of matter. So when opposites attract, or opposite sexes attract, they show that matter matters even in relationships.

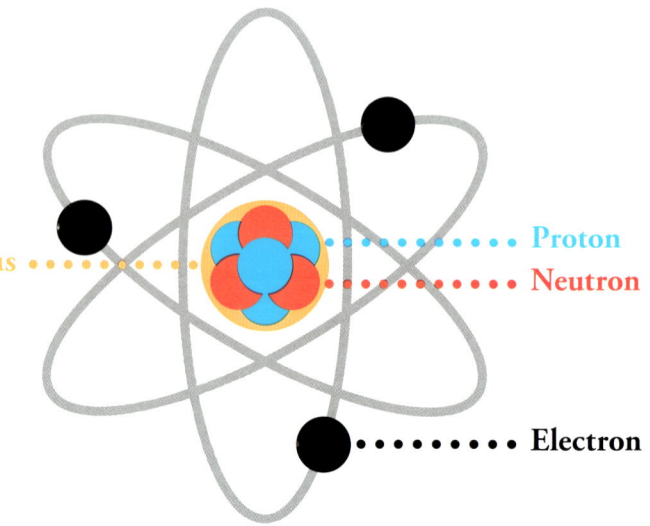

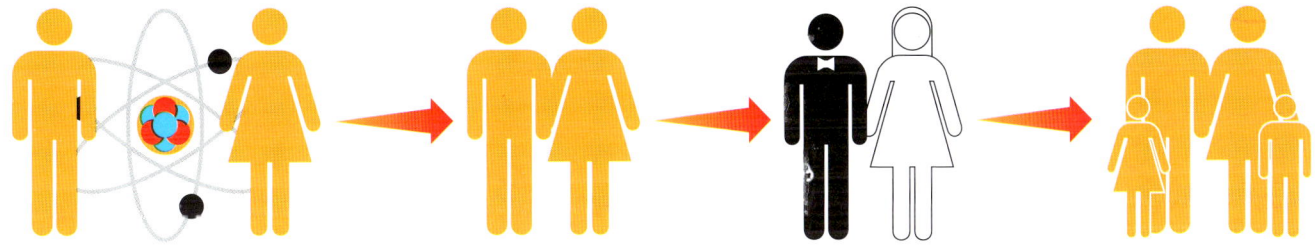

The Good News of Attraction

God created attraction so that families would be formed. A husband and wife experience deep peace through their vows, and then they procreate with God. Those children, who deserve to be the fruit of committed love, then have the guidance and security of loving parents. This pathway to peace and parenthood allows for real love, instead of the counterfeit kind. This means attraction is good news, because it sets them on the path to real love.

When you experience the feelings of attraction, it is good to be aware of this path of real love and examine the inner movements of your heart. Girls: being attracted to boys is God's way of calling you one day to be a wife and mother one day (or a spiritual wife and mother). Boys: being attracted to girls is God's way of calling you one day to be a husband and father one day (or a spiritual husband and father). This is good news!

"**THE TRUTH OF LOVE**, which is proclaimed by the Song of Songs, cannot be separated from the 'language of the body.' ...This is also the truth of the increasing *closeness of the spouses*, which grows through love...." *Theology of the Body 111:1*

Aardvark, Alien, or Adam?

Does Scripture help us to understand attraction? St. John Paul observes that Adam and Eve experienced holy desire, or attraction. What did that look like?

Remember, before Eve was created, Adam named all of the animals, but "none was a suitable helpmate" (Gen. 2:20). God cast Adam into a deep sleep. When Adam awoke, he saw Eve and cried out, "Bone of my bone and flesh of my flesh" (Gen. 2:23). In other words, there was chemistry! He sang out his excitement because he knew, at last, that he belonged to **her**. How did he know? By her human body. (She was not an aardvark, or an orangutan, or an alien, or a robot!)

Adam and Eve also knew they were created **for** each other. How did they know? Adam and Eve saw their bodies rightly, as a revelation of the whole person. Therefore, they knew that they were gifts to each other because his male body and her female body were complementary.

Seeing the Whole Person

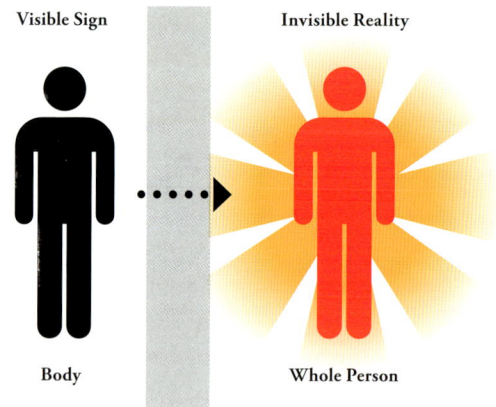

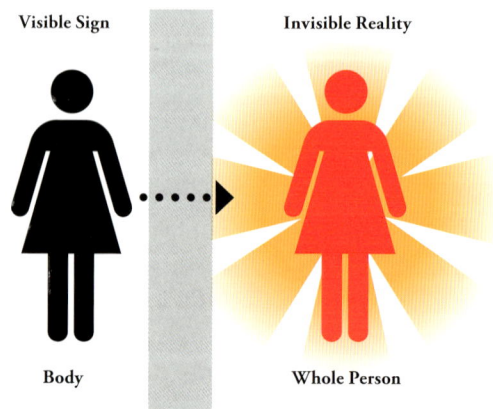

Based on *TOB* 12:4-13:1; 14:2-4. © Copyright 2018 by Monica Ashour. All rights reserved.

"...[T]he key moment [was when, in the human] heart, doubt was cast on the Gift."
Theology of the Body 26:4

God made the body as a "sacrament"; the body reveals the whole person. We all have invisible qualities—hopes and dreams, personality and character, humor and quirks—revealed through the body. Adam was aware of Eve's entire self, and Eve was aware of Adam's entire self.

Unfortunately, this sacramental vision of the body became corrupted. Adam and Eve believed the Deceiver who convinced them that God was a tyrant. In their hearts, they doubted God's gift of the law of love and believed the counterfeit. Sin had entered their hearts even before their bodily actions followed. They ate the forbidden fruit and then hid from God in shame. They did not evaluate the inner movements of their hearts, and each started to see the other as an object for use.

The result of Adam and Eve's fall was division. Previously, they had known the security of true love. Now, they doubted not just God, but each other.

The Heart: Where Sin Begins

"You have heard that it was said, 'You shall not commit adultery.' But I say to you, everyone who looks at a woman with lust has already committed adultery with her in his heart. —Mt. 5:27-28

Love vs. Lust

Sadly, when sin entered the world, humans began to view each other as objects instead of as whole persons. What was the result? The "other" became merely a means to an end, or a way to achieve selfish goals. When lust is given free rein, attraction becomes self-centered. It leads to loneliness, heartache, pain, and broken relationships. In other words, lust is a counterfeit for love. True attraction, governed by virtue, leads to real love.

God gave us feelings of guilt and shame to alert us to lust. If you feel shame, know that you are being drawn to the mercy of the cross. However, shame does not define who you are. Forgiveness and mercy are the reasons Jesus died for you. Repent and start over. You are **not** your sin; you are the brother or sister of Jesus and the son or daughter of God the Father and the temple of the Holy Spirit.

Love vs. Lust

Love	Lust
Giving the gift of self	**Taking** for oneself
Respects the body as some**one**	Sees the body as some**thing**
Sacrifices **oneself for others**	Sacrifices **others for oneself**
Yearns for **eternal** joy	Grasps at **fleeting** pleasure
Liberates us	**Enslaves** us

This is a modified version of a diagram by Christoper West, MTS. Used with permission. © Copyright 2018 by Monica Ashour. All rights reserved.

Preparing for Real Love Now

We are all made for real love—not just for attraction, and certainly not for lust. Even within the Sacrament of Matrimony, attraction must be purified. But discernment of marriage is for later. So what can you do in the meantime?

Start by deepening each and every one of your relationships now. Be intentional about living **for** others. When you do so, you establish a foundation for your future vocation. Meanwhile, keep in mind that everyBODY is made for love. EveryBODY can give the gift of self.

Since God created us **for** each other, just as Eve was **for** Adam and Adam was **for** Eve, you can be **for** the people around you. You and your teammates are **for** each other. Brothers and sisters are **for** each other. Teachers are **for** their students, and you can be **for** your teachers.

"[All of history is determined by...] 'who' she shall be for him and he for her."
Theology of the Body 43:7

We Are Made for Relationships

son for father and mother	**daughter** for father and mother
brother for brother/sister	**sister** for brother/sister
husband for wife	**wife** for husband
father for son/daughter	**mother** for son/daughter
friend for friend	**friend** for friend
nephew for uncle/aunt	**niece** for uncle/aunt
uncle for nephew/niece	**aunt** for nephew/niece
coach for players	**coach** for players
student for teachers	**student** for teachers

© Copyright 2020 by Monica Ashour. All rights reserved.

Brothers and Sisters

In your present stage of life, how can you practice real—not counterfeit—love with those around you? Think about it this way: girls, you hope the best for your brother, even if he might get on your nerves. Boys, even though you may fight with your sister, you would never want anyone to be cruel to her. If you had to, wouldn't you ultimately die for a sibling if he or she were in danger? That is called sacrificial love.

With this in mind, here is some advice: a boy should learn to see every girl as a sister, and a girl should see every boy as a brother, before they think about dating. When boys and girls see each other as brothers and sisters, they recognize their shared humanity. They understand that they are equals, though distinct. Most importantly, they know that they are both made for love and not for use.

The LORD God then built the rib that he had taken from the man into a woman. Gen. 2:22

Based on Song of Songs and *TOB* 109:3-110:4. © Copyright 2018 by Monica Ashour. All rights reserved.

Guarding Your Heart

In the Theology of the Body, St. John Paul lays the groundwork for true and lasting relationships. By giving generous, sacrificial gifts of self to your family and friends now, you are preparing yourself for lifelong friendships and for your future vocation.

As you practice real love, you will find certain people attractive. Crushes are normal, so do not be alarmed or "crushed" by them. But even though attraction is God-given, refrain from becoming a couple too quickly.

This does **not** mean you should shut people out, but be very careful in giving away your heart since you are still learning who you are.

Your decisions now can impact your whole life and affect other people too. So, work for the good of others and keep striving toward the goal of real love.

Points to Ponder:
1. How can you practice seeing everyBODY as a whole person? Explain how this perspective helps you to live for others and avoid using them.
2. What are some practical ways you can see your "crushes" as brothers or sisters?

Mission:
Girls: Every time you see a boy, think to yourself, "He is my brother."
Boys: Every time you see a girl, think to yourself, "She is my sister."

Keep doing this until it becomes second nature.

3. The Sacred One-Flesh Union

By now you know three basic, guiding principles of Theology of the Body:
- Real love is the gift of self.
- The body speaks a language.
- Holiness begins with the heart.

Now let's examine these in the light of **sexuality**. Here is a true story based on a couple who found real love by following these principles.

A Love Story

Patrick and Rebecca met in college and felt immediate chemistry. Having grown up in Catholic homes, they both knew that chastity was a virtue. However, they developed bad habits due to the influence of the disordered culture. Patrick had been caught up in using others, and Rebecca had difficulty with her self-worth, which put her in danger of being used. Unfortunately, they gave in to sex outside of marriage. Afterward, they felt shame and remorse.

Yet, such guilt led them to find out the truth of sexuality and led to their conversion. Patrick and Rebecca attended a talk on the Theology of the Body. There they learned about the design and purpose of their human bodies. For the first time, they understood the God-given truth about attraction, love, and sexuality. It changed their lives.

Patrick realized that he was not viewing Rebecca as a whole person, deserving of honor and real love. Rebecca, in turn, saw that she was using Patrick to fulfill her need for self-worth. When Patrick understood that marriage is the proper context to express sacred sexual love, he repented, getting on his knees to pray… and then, within a few months, he again got down on his knee and proposed to Rebecca! She was able to receive Patrick's proposal and responded with a resounding "Yes!" since she, too, had begun to trust God and see her own worth. They were now ready to give the **gift of self** authentically.

Living the Gift of Self

As newlyweds, Patrick and Rebecca lived out the **giving-receiving-fruitfulness** imprint of God. They shared their love of cooking, camping, and ski trips together. On any given day, friends would join them in a house full of food, laughter, and conversation, all of which was the fruitfulness of their relationship.

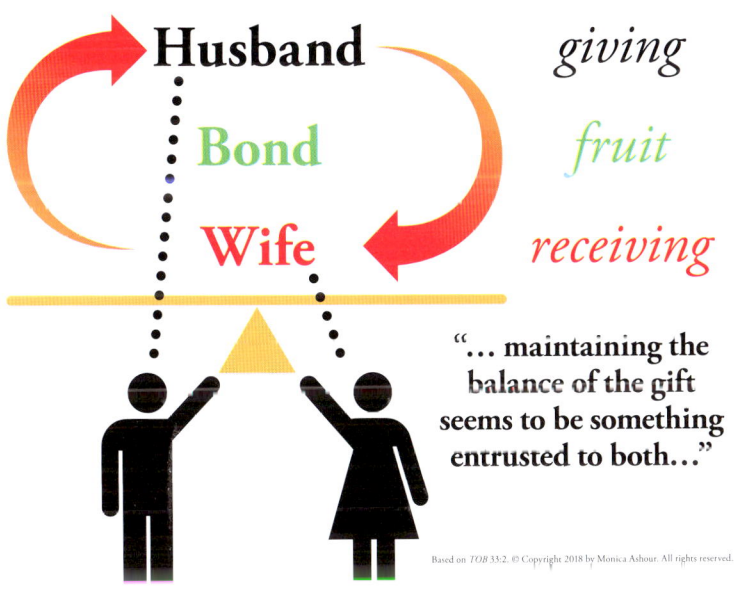

Giving and Receiving Balance

"… maintaining the balance of the gift seems to be something entrusted to both…"

When there is a balance of giving and receiving, love naturally expands. Not only were Patrick and Rebecca open to their friends, but they were open to bearing and raising children. They were overjoyed when they found out that Rebecca was pregnant. To them, it was as if their love was so strong, it had become its own person—their child!

Sometimes when one is open to a life of love, God widens the heart. Patrick and Rebecca now have six children. Their fifth child, Paul, has very special needs. He cannot see, walk, or speak. But rather than feeling sorry for themselves, Patrick and Rebecca have received the mystery of the gift of Paul. They realize that he cements their family bond through their sacrificial love for him. Paul bonds the family together in a special way.

The Marital Language of the Body

Let's apply the second basic concept of Theology of the Body—the body speaks a language—to sexuality. Remember that **certain bodily actions mean certain things**—our bodies are to communicate truth. A smile communicates welcome, and a punch signifies aggression.

Then what is the meaning of marital intercourse? Through the language of the body, sex means, "I'm married to you. I'm devoted to you for my entire life. Our loving, holy union may bring forth a new life—a baby—to our family."

The Deep Meaning of Sexual Love

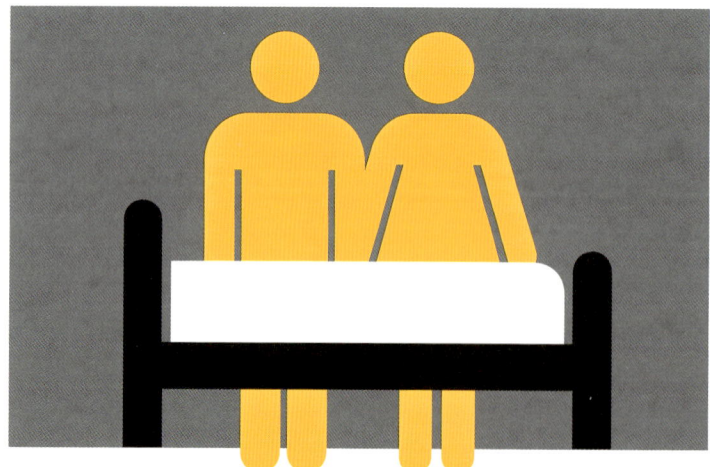

"I am yours, and you are mine.
We are married,
and I'm ready to have a child with you."

Based on *TOB* 123:1, *TOB* 125:1; *TOB* 127:1; *Humanae Vitae* 13. © Copyright 2018 by Monica Ashour. All rights reserved.

Given the deep meaning of married love, what a shock it is for those who are sexually active before marriage to discover they have been telling a lie with their bodies! When Rebecca and Patrick first discovered the Theology of the Body and the truth of the meaning of sex, they realized that their intimacy before marriage had betrayed truth. They had fallen for counterfeit love. Without them realizing it, sex had meant giving in to lust and self-gratification. Humbled, they asked each other for forgiveness and went to Confession to start living the truth anew.

Practicing Purity

Waiting until marriage is not a random rule meant to make life difficult. God designed sexual union so that within the context of marriage, it is an expression of real love. In the act of marital union and communion, the bodies of husband and wife say: "I love you, my beloved spouse. I give to you my whole self as a gift and receive from you your whole self as a gift." By waiting until marriage, they acknowledge that the body speaks a language, they respect its truth and, moreover, they experience real love.

"Sexuality, in which [human persons'] belonging to the bodily and biological world is expressed, becomes personal and truly human when it is integrated into the relationship of one person to another, in the complete and lifelong mutual gift of a man and a woman."

CCC 2337

Sacred Altar & Sacred Bed

Let's examine the Sacrament of Matrimony even further. At their wedding, a couple speaks the truth of their love before God and each other at the sacred altar. They first speak their vows with the language of words.

Then, on their wedding night, they repeat those vows again, this time with the language of the body to express the sacred one-flesh union. When the language of the body matches the language of words, a couple is living out sexual integrity.

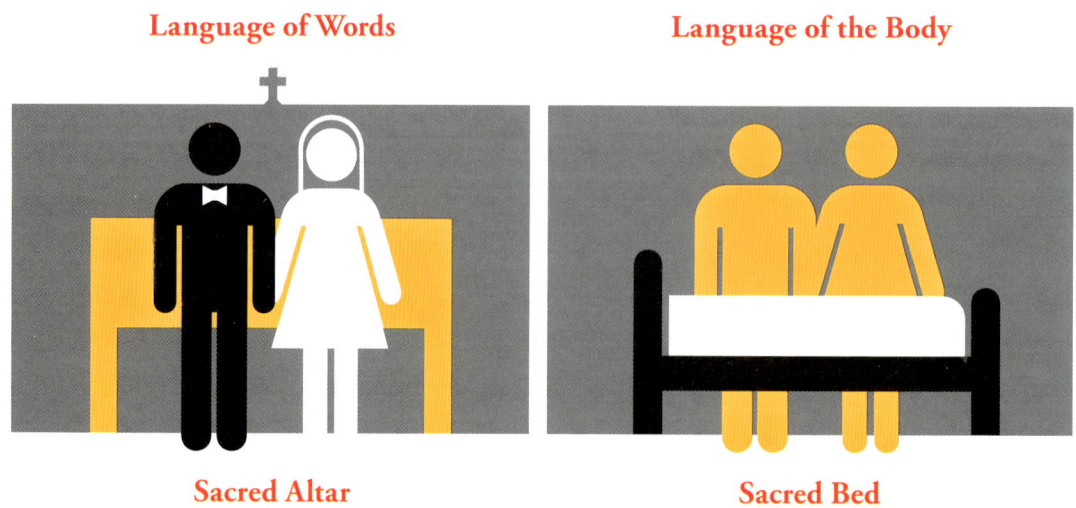

From *TOB* 117b:6. © Copyright 2018 by Monica Ashour. All rights reserved.

Patrick and Rebecca know that every time they come together in marital love, they renew their wedding vows. The marital language of their bodies tells the truth and reminds them of their sacramental union in every aspect of their lives.

Did you know that when a husband and wife express their love through sexual union according to God's design, it is a holy and chaste act? Chastity is the proper ordering of sexuality according to one's state of life, and chastity frees people for real, not counterfeit, love.

What about those who are already sexually active and are learning the truth of love and purity for the first time? They often have regrets and say, "Why didn't we learn this as teenagers? We've been doing things all wrong. Now what do we do?"

We can tell them, "Be not afraid; there is hope and healing." Anyone can ask forgiveness for any sin. That's why Jesus died—not to condemn us but to **free** us for real love. Anyone who has fallen can start again, living the truth of the body and the truth of love. Confession is a beautiful way to experience mercy, forgiveness, healing, and a new start.

You might be wondering why people should be chaste if they can be forgiven. The pain, heartache, and deep-seated wounds of sexual impurity will make it more difficult for real love in the future. Living the **language of the body** in truth brings happiness and security.

"[Do not] judge, and you will not be judged. [Do not] condemn, and you will not be condemned. Forgive and you will be forgiven." *Lk. 6:37*

Holiness and Sexuality

Now let's turn to our final foundational truth, **holiness**, and see how it applies to sexuality. Remember: **The truth that you know is the truth you should show.** To live out Theology of the Body is to "own" God's truth of love in your heart and to match your bodily actions to it.

If a boy sees an attractive girl and is able to appreciate her beauty in gratitude without dwelling on sexual thoughts, he is practicing holiness. He is becoming a Theology of the Body man like Patrick.

If a girl meets an attractive boy and is able to appreciate his strength and charm without trying to attract him with seduction or mind games, she is practicing holiness. She is becoming a Theology of the Body woman like Rebecca.

Matters of the Mature Heart

Becoming a Theology of the Body man or woman does not happen overnight, for it requires practice as you mature. How can you be holy? First and foremost, do you "own" God's truth in your heart? What does that mean? Little children simply obey rules, often without understanding why.

But as you mature, you learn to examine the truth, accept it, live it, and even defend it. That is called **owning** the truth.

Owning the truth helps you be aware of your inner impulses. It also helps you to evaluate them. When a mature couple dates, the right impulse for each person is to will the good of the other. If temptations to sin arise, they know that they deserve better. They look beyond their mere (though good) feelings of desire to find out the inner motives of their hearts. Just as gold-miners dig deeply into the earth for treasure, the dating couple can dig into the depth of their hearts for the truth.

On the next page, notice that as you dig deeper into the earth (your heart), you move closer to truth and to real love. Truth is golden!

"Blessed are the [pure] of heart, for they will see God."   *Mt. 5:8*

Mining the Greatest Truth of Love

As we dig deeper into our hearts, we find the deepest truths.

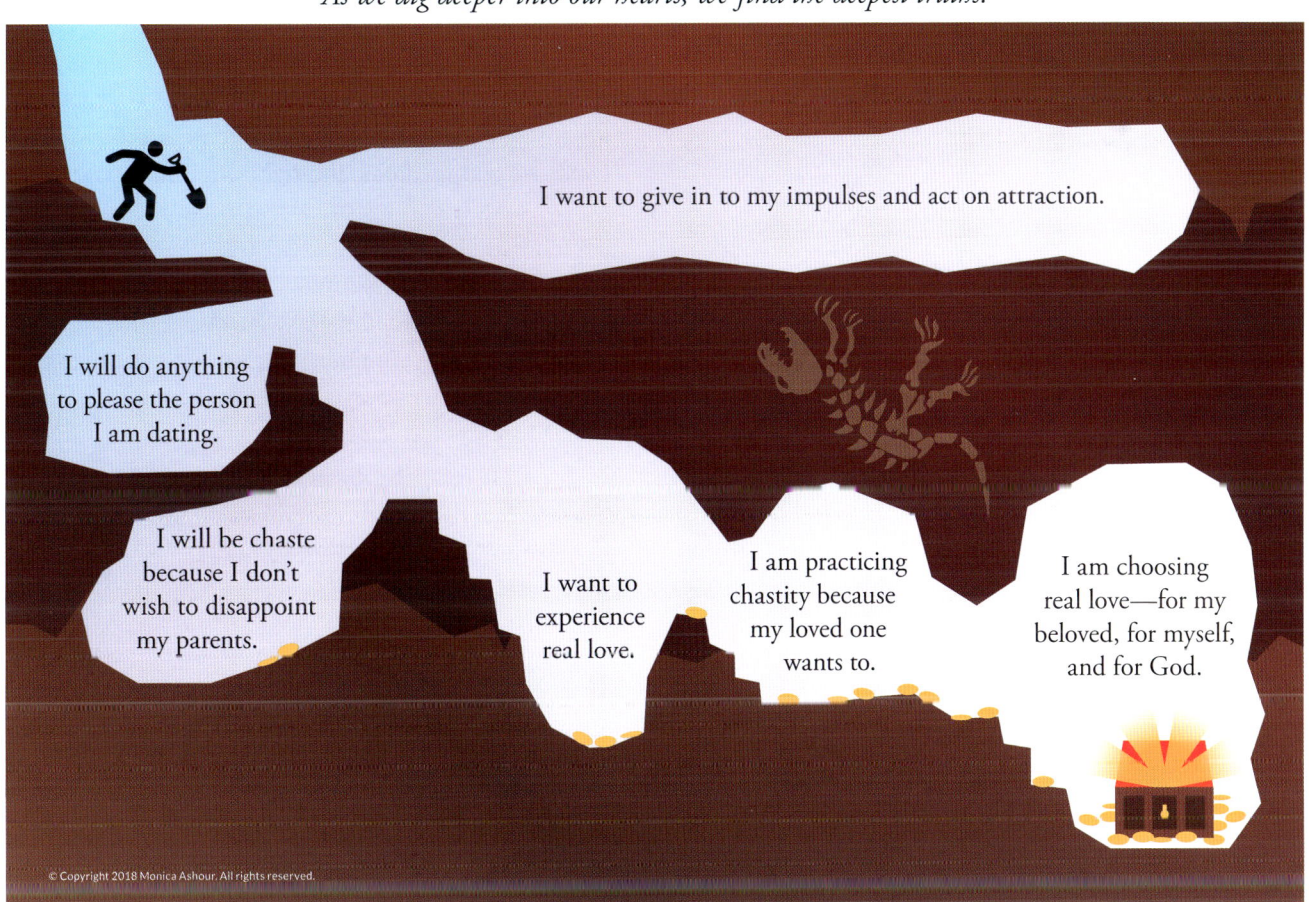

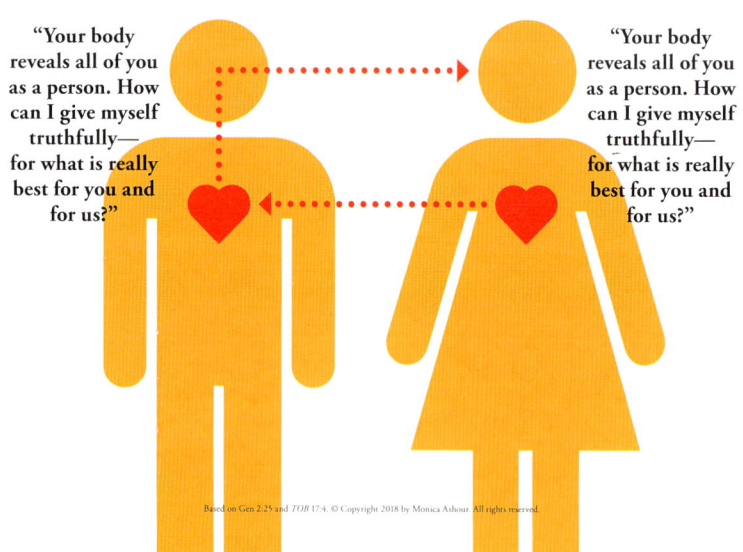

Those who are striving for real, rather than counterfeit, love must train themselves to be "gold-miners of the heart." As they sift through its inner movements, they may find fool's gold, a sad counterfeit. But if they ask for a pure heart and a pure view, God can help them find the real gold of authentic love.

Reaching the treasure of real love doesn't happen overnight. Patrick and Rebecca can attest to that. When people are in the clutches of sin, it can be difficult to break free. Patrick and Rebecca met Jesus and found forgiveness in the Sacrament of Confession. They also made a habit of praying with each other, asking God to protect them from counterfeit love. In addition, they surrounded themselves with friends who were also on the path to purity.

"...[T]he inner man is *called by Christ to reach a more mature and complete evaluation that allows him to distinguish and judge the various movements of his own heart.* One should add that this task can be carried out and that it is truly worthy of man."

Theology of the Body 48:4

Maturing to Love

The first step toward mature love in the area of sexuality is being aware of the inner movements of your heart. Take a look at the following diagram. Perhaps the boy is **not** aware of his lust, nor the girl aware that she seeks to use him. Their immaturity cannot lead to real love.

Perhaps they **are** aware, but they don't care. Sadly, this kind of counterfeit love causes heartache and wounds.

St. John Paul reminds us that the Holy Spirit, Who forms "an alliance with the human spirit," can purify our hearts and help us make our bodily actions consistent with the truth of love.

"[Jesus] said to them, 'You justify yourselves in the sight of others, but God knows your hearts....'" *Lk. 16:15*

33

From Feelings to Friendship

What is it like to fall in love? The feelings of being in love are exciting and can lead to the real thing. But feelings alone are fleeting and unreliable, whereas real love opens the door to deep and lasting delight.

Read the diagram on this page from left to right. You see that attraction is the starting point. But notice what is between attraction and marriage—friendship. Slowing down your attraction and just being friends builds a more solid relationship. It reins in strong desires and allows real love to blossom.

Group dates, hobbies, arts, sports, and conversation can all solidify similar values and build a relationship based on real love. Notice the foundation of this diagram in gold. Self-sacrificial love is the result of living out the three basic Theology of the Body principles. It is a great preparation for your future.

The Purification of Love

"So-called 'safe sex'... is actually, in view of the overall requirements of the person, radically not safe, indeed it is extremely dangerous. It endangers both the person and the family. What is this danger? It is the loss of truth about one's own self and about the family, together with the risk of a loss of freedom and consequently of a loss of love itself." *Letter to Families*

A New Kind of Revolution

It started with a T.V. documentary about female models. For one photo shoot, models endure hours of make-up, only then to be heavily altered in image editing software. As a result, advertisements give merely a counterfeit version of beauty. A group of seven college students from St. Mary's Catholic Center at Texas A&M University found this highly disturbing and began meeting to plan how to raise awareness of counterfeit cultural messages.

Then they discovered Theology of the Body. They felt led by the Holy Spirit to create The Revolution, which teaches Theology of the Body to college students. One event, "Unveiling Reality," presents the reality of lust and emotional wounds resulting from "safe sex." Then, it encourages living the truth of the body and sexual integrity. Thousands attended this event. Many participants now have happy marriages, founded on purity and the mutual gift of self. Others have entered the priesthood and consecrated life. The truth of real love transforms!

Stephanie & Christopher Lafitte, co-founders of The Revolution

Let's summarize the basics of Theology of the Body as well as their application to the area of sexuality.

The Body Matters

Topic	Body: All Humans	Body: Sexuality
Gift of Self Giving, receiving, and fruit	"I choose to talk to my parents and not use them for money so that our relationship will grow."	"I care so much about the person I like—I will not be sexually active, for it is use."
Language of the Body Integrity of words and actions	Smile = "Nice to meet you!" Push = "Get away from me!"	Sexual intimacy = "I am yours forever; we are married and ready to be parents."
Holiness Pure heart + bodily actions	"I know gossiping is wrong—with my body, I will not gossip."	"I know sexual actions outside marriage are wrong—with my body, I will live chastely."
Femininity Free to thrive as a woman	"I will work on virtue to be a gift for others in my femininity."	"My body is a sacrament of my femininity. I will live chastely for my sake and for the person I like."
Masculinity Free to thrive as a man	"I will work on virtue to be a gift for others in my masculinity."	"My body is a sacrament of my masculinity. I will live chastely for my sake and for the person I like."

© Copyright 2020 by Monica Ashour. All rights reserved.

The Truth of Matrimony

Bearing Witness to Love

Ultimately, you are made to bring Heaven to bear on the Earth. When you practice self-sacrificial love toward your family and friends, teachers and coaches, classmates and siblings—everyBODY—you are bringing them God's love. Remember, do not fall for the counterfeit, but choose real love by living out the truth of the body. That is the foundation for real, marital love. You are preparing your heart for and loving a person you have not even met yet: your future spouse!

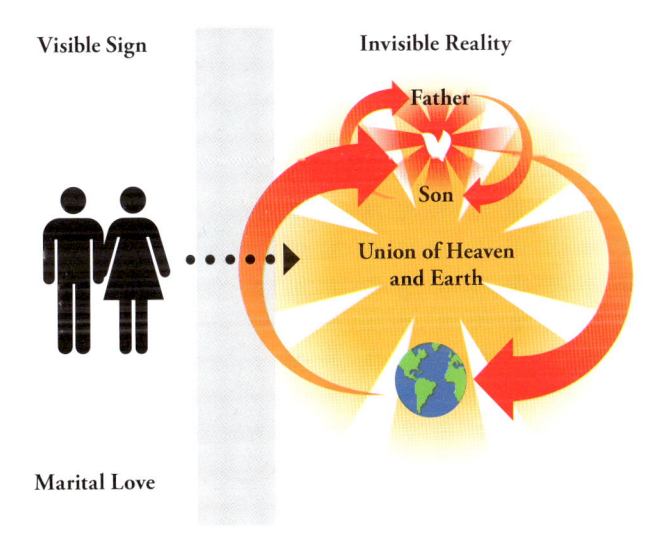

Visible Sign — Marital Love

Invisible Reality — Father, Son, Union of Heaven and Earth

Based on *TOB* 13:2-4; 16:3-19:6; 93:1-7; 117b:6. © Copyright 2018 by Monica Ashour. All rights reserved.

Points to Ponder:
1. What is sexual integrity? How is it different from counterfeit cultural messages?
2. What steps can you take to own the truth in your heart? How can you better notice your heart's "inner movements" and then learn to "evaluate" them?

Mission: Notice the inner movements of your heart that are good. Notice which ones lead to lust. In your prayer time, tell Jesus about both, and ask Him to help you find real love.

4 Identity and Vocation

Who Am I?

These three Theology of the Body principles are a basic recipe: the gift of self, the language of the body spoken in truth, and holiness! The combination of these three ingredients yields purity for each of us.

These principles also bring you closer to answering the biggest question in your life right now: "Who am I?" At your age, striving for self-knowledge and understanding your identity are hugely important. Do not stop your search with "What do I feel like?" Feelings are unreliable and can complicate the issue. Identity is foundational and is tied to the truth of the body. It is grounded in relationships. Who are you in relationship to God and to others? Let's see how the Theology of the Body can help you find some answers.

A Real Boy

Do you know the story of Pinocchio? From his first day of school, the wooden puppet falls into sins of pride, greed, and selfish pleasure. When his loving father, Geppetto, tries to rescue him, Geppetto is swallowed by a whale. Pinocchio, in turn, sacrifices himself trying to save his father. After pulling Geppetto into a cave and saving his life, Pinocchio weakens and dies. Suddenly, the Blue Fairy appears and changes Pinocchio into a real boy.

You may think Pinocchio is just for children, but a deep, Theology of the Body meaning lies within this narrative. Though Pinocchio began with a pure heart, the lies of the world began to chip away at the truth he knew. He soon became enslaved and lost his freedom. It wasn't until he learned sacrificial love that he found his identity—his authentic self.

Gift of Self + Truthful Language of the Body + Holiness = PURITY

The Truth about Love

Let's explore how **truth** leads you to know who you are. Think about a time when someone lied to you. Did you get angry? Why? Lies anger us because we are made for truth.

What are some of the lies that society teaches about sexuality? One dangerous lie is that love equals sex. That would mean that no one could experience love unless it were expressed sexually.

But everyBODY is made for real love. Love is not limited to sexuality; it encompasses much more.

You will also hear many messages in the culture that will try to convince you that sex outside of marriage is real love. This is a lie because real love is inseparable from the truth of our design.

People cannot live without love.

Path to Truth → **Love = Gift of Self** → **People cannot live without the Gift of Self.**

False Path → **Love = sex** → **People cannot live without sex.**

"Man cannot live without love. He remains a being that is incomprehensible for himself, his life is senseless if love is not revealed to him...."   *The Redeemer of Man*

Love Leads to Freedom

Why is freedom so important to who you are? Without freedom, you cannot love. And you can only find yourself through an authentic gift of self, which is a free choice. When you have self-mastery over your sexual desires, you will have freedom over those desires rather than being enslaved to them. You are in charge! St. John Paul's Theology of the Body can be summed up in this thought: **the gift of freedom is for the freedom of the gift**. In other words, free will is for love.

Love must be free. And just as you can be trapped in counterfeit "love," you can also be trapped in counterfeit "freedom." Many people think freedom means you can do whatever you want, whenever you want. This is not true freedom. Such "freedom" is called license and seeks selfish, temporary excitement. In this chart, the right side might feel like freedom at first, but it is actually anarchy, which is lawlessness. Such sin bows to one's selfish whims and desires.

Freedom vs. License

Freedom	License
Freedom **from** compulsion	"Freedom" **to indulge** compulsions
Freedom **from** sin	"Freedom" **to** sin
Do what **is** good	Do what **feels** good
Sees **sin** as the tyrant	Sees **law** as the tyrant
Law is **written on the heart**	Law feels **imposed**
Fulfills the law	**Breaks** the law
Choice **between** good and evil	**Any** choice is a good choice
Affirms love	**Negates** love

Real freedom seeks the truth and the good of others, which is called the "common good." If a teen decided he was "free" to do drugs because it's his life after all, would he be the only one affected? No. It would take an emotional and financial toll on his parents, and his siblings would be confused and saddened. Not only do we hurt ourselves, but we hurt others when we mistake license for freedom. Rather, we are meant to be free from sin so that we can be free for love. Sin enslaves; love frees.

Based on chart by Christopher West, MTS. Used with permission. © Copyright 2018 by Monica Ashour. All rights reserved.

> **"The perfection of Christian life is measured… by the measure of love."**
> *Theology of the Body 78:3*

Your Deepest Identity

Can you answer the questions "Who am I?" or "What is my identity?" You are given your deepest identity when you are baptized. That is the moment you become your heavenly Father's son or daughter. He will love you no matter what. Your identity as son or daughter of the King cannot be taken from you. It does not matter if you are made fun of, or if you fight with your parents, or if you make a low grade. No matter what, your true identity as God's child remains. In turn, you are called to love others, for love enriches your identity, forming more of who you are.

As you grow older, you have the freedom to build on that calling to love. "To be called" is what *vocation* means; everybody's vocation is the same: to love.

Vocations typically take one of two paths. The natural path that God calls most men and women to follow is marriage. Why? Love. He calls some along the other path—the one leading to priesthood or religious life. Why? Love. All vocations have the same destination: love. The good news of the body is that we are made **for** love **by** Love.

Vows and Freedom

Some might think that taking a vow restricts who you are and limits your freedom. Paradoxically, vows **add to** freedom. How does that work? What if you could choose from among hundreds of video games, and each day you played a different one? Because your attention is spread so thin, you would not master any of them.

Too many choices lead to disrupted attention and focus, whereas a single choice allows you to excel in one area. This is true when it comes to vowed commitments as well. Rather than fickle emotions determining choices, wedding vows free you to focus your love on your spouse and family first. In turn, your family can reach out to others.

Vow to Vow: Baptismal Vow to Vocational Vow

Vow of Marriage
"I promise to be committed to you, my spouse, Freely, Fully, Faithfully, and Fruitfully."

Vow of Celibacy for the Kingdom
"I promise to be committed to you, my Church, Freely, Fully, Faithfully, and Fruitfully."

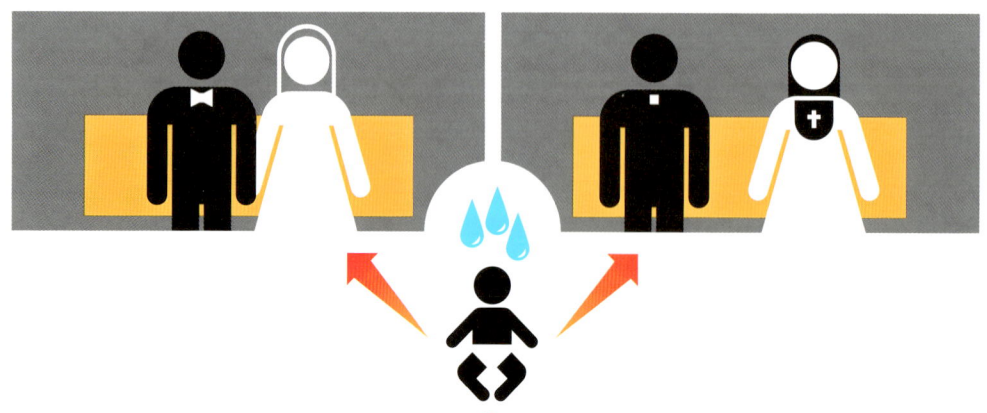

Vow of Baptism
"I promise to be committed to you, Jesus—and Your Church, Freely, Fully, Faithfully, and Fruitfully."

Counterfeit vs. True Love

Those called to be priests or consecrated also give the gift of self through the body in a different way than married people do, and their fruitfulness is beyond question. The life they bring the world is the truth of eternal life—they teach us to look beyond this world to the next. Furthermore, their vows of chastity, poverty, and obedience guide all of us toward freedom.

From Fallen to Free

Fallen Nature	Redeemed Nature
Lust Concupiscence of the FLESH	**Chastity** Free to LOVE
Greed Concupiscence of the EYES	**Poverty** Free to GIVE
Pride Concupiscence of the PRIDE OF LIFE	**Obedience** Free to SERVE

Based on 1 Jn 2:15-16, *CCC* 2337 and *TOB* 46:2. © Copyright 2018 by Monica Ashour. All rights reserved.

St. John Paul points out that each vocation—marriage and continence for the kingdom—"mirrors" the other. For instance, marriage is rightly **exclusive** on Earth; therefore, married spouses serve as a reminder to priests and religious that they belong **exclusively** to Christ. Here we find a beautiful symmetry.

On the other hand, continence for the kingdom is rightly **inclusive**. Those who take consecrated vows are meant to reach out to all people. They point to a heavenly future when God will be our "all in all" (1 Cor 15:28), and we will be united, together with the saints and angels. Priests and religious remind married people to avoid a life dedicated only to each other, but to be open to **including** those beyond the immediate family. In other words, the family has a mission to help the world! Love for fruitful union is the purpose of both vocations.

Free, Full, Faithful, and Fruitful

So, how do you find your truest identity? It has to do with learning to love. Look at how Jesus and Mary speak the language of love: freely, fully, faithfully, and fruitfully.

Jesus' Loving Heart

The truth of love centers around the **body**, the Body of Jesus Christ on the cross. Over 2,000 years ago Jesus Christ offered his total Gift of Self on Calvary. By doing so, He showed us how to love—freely, fully, faithfully, and fruitfully. He **freely** and willingly accepted death for us and was not coerced or forced to do so. He gave Himself **fully** without holding anything back as He entered into His suffering for us. **Faithfully**, He did not waver from His mission to save us. Finally, He brought about abundant, new divine life offered to us all as the **fruit**. Our covenant with the Father is restored. Jesus on the cross makes the ultimate Gift of Love.

All Love Comes from the Heart of God

For a whole heart… you need each part

Based on Fr. Hans Urs von Balthasar's *The Heart of the World* and *Humanae Vitae*, 9. © Copyright 2014 by Monica Ashour. All rights reserved.

Mary's Loving Heart

Since Jesus gives the Gift of Self on the cross, who is there to receive Him? That's where Mary's identity comes in. Mary was not forced to be the Mother of God, nor was she forced to be at the crucifixion; she **freely** loved throughout her entire life by saying "Yes" to God's grace.

Mary received so **fully** that she is called "full of grace." She **faithfully** adhered to God's will throughout her entire life, and she bore the greatest **fruit**—Jesus Himself. Moreover, since we are brothers and sisters of Christ, Mary is our Mother too! She teaches us to love her Son.

> **"From Mary, we learn to trust even when all hope seems gone. From Mary, we learn to love Christ, her Son and the Son of God."**
> *St. John Paul, Homily on October 6, 1979*

How to Be Like Jesus and Mary

How might you as young men and women also co-create yourselves with God? That's a complex way of asking, "What kind of person do you want to be?" By making decisions based on the model of Jesus' and Mary's free, full, faithful, fruitful love, you will find your true identity.

Free

You can work on self-mastery so you are not enslaved to sin.

> *Instead of exploding in anger at your parents or siblings, stay calm. You are not enslaved to anger and extreme emotions.*

Full

Be "all-in" so you can offer a total gift of self.

> *Be attentive and not half-hearted when listening to someone speak. Ask yourself whether your electronic devices distract from your full attention.*

Faithful

Keep your word so you can be trusted.

> *If you commit to doing an activity, stay with it. Tell the truth with the language of words and the language of your body.*

Fruitful

Let your kindness overflow into the lives of others.

> *Invite those who are often left out. Offer up your sufferings for others who need your prayers.*

Reverence and Purity

As a way to live out purity, St. John Paul emphasizes that we are to cultivate **reverence**. When you are reverent toward a person, you will see him or her as a whole person, deserving of love, not as an object for use.

If you find yourself attracted to someone, practice reverence. You will be drawn toward that person in wonder, but you will be held back by proper awe so as not to use or violate his or her mystery.

Boys, one day you will be ready to pursue a woman or perhaps you will discern the priesthood and/or religious life. In either vocation, you are to be reverent "as the guardian of the mystery… of the gift" (Theology of the Body 19:2).

Girls, whether as a consecrated sister or married woman, see others with reverence, including yourself. As a child of God, you deserve reverence. You are the "master of your mystery" (Theology of the Body 110:7).

How do you practice reverence now? Through the gift of self. Your gift of self (by giving or receiving) will develop a sense of reverence.
- If a teacher needs help with a problem, be the first to volunteer to help her.
- If your dad or mom is too tired to make dinner, offer to help in the kitchen.
- If your brother wants to play a game but you wanted to play another, choose his game instead.

When you seek out ways to be a gift to others, you will sense reverence growing in your heart.

"The reverence born in [a person] for everything bodily and sexual, both in himself and in every other human being, male and female, turns out to be the most essential power for keeping the body 'with holiness.'"
Theology of the Body 54:4

The Gift of the Holy Spirit

The good news is that you are not alone in your fight for purity! Mary's example witnesses to us that it is possible to be pure. If we fall, remember that Jesus is the Divine Physician who sends the Holy Spirit, like a scalpel, into our hearts. Eradicating lust may seem as serious as heart surgery, but forgiveness, healing, and mercy are the right medicines.

God through His Church wants to promote, preserve, and purify your love. With His grace, everyBODY can live out purity and find real love.

The Power of the Holy Spirit

use — *detachment*
lust — *sin*
selfishness — *temptation*

Love, Joy, Peace, Patience, Kindness, Generosity, Gentleness, Self-Control, Faithfulness
Gal 5:22

"…[Behind] these moral virtues stands a *specific choice*, that is, an effort of the will, a *fruit of the human spirit* permeated by the Spirit of God… man proves to be *stronger thanks to the power of the Holy Spirit, who*, working within the human spirit, causes *its desires to bear fruit in the good*."
TOB 51:6

Based on *TOB 51*. © Copyright 2013 by Monica Ashour. All rights reserved.

Points to Ponder:
1. What do you need to consider in your search for identity? What is your deepest identity?
2. How do vows bring freedom to the vocations of marriage or continence for the kingdom?

Mission: St. Catherine of Siena said that if everyone lived God's design for love, the world would be set ablaze with Christ's love. Be full of love so you can set the world ablaze!